Job Interview Success

Impress Employers and Land Your Dream Job

Table of Contents

Chapter 1. Introduction

Get ready to transform your job interview game! Our Special Report on "Job Interview Success: Impress Employers and Land Your Dream Job" is designed to be your ultimate guide to not just surviving, but thriving in any job interview scenario. Whether you are an entry-level aspirant or an experienced professional, we've harvested effective strategies, compiled industry insights, and aggregated expert advice to ensure you shine in the spotlight. It's your turn to impress employers and grab the reins of your dream career. So why wait? Let's embark on this journey together and turn those interview jitters into a palpable enthusiasm. This Special Report will equip you, inspire you, and make your job interview success a reality! Let's jumpstart your journey to landing that dream job!

Chapter 2. Understanding the Anatomy of a Job Interview

The job interview process isn't particularly mysterious or unpredictable. It possesses a structure—an anatomy—that can be broken down, understood, and leveraged to your advantage. Going into an interview without knowledge of this anatomy would be akin to trying to assemble a jigsaw puzzle without seeing the picture on the box. Let's demystify the process.

2.1. The Basic Framework

Every job interview, regardless of industry, position, or level of experience of the candidate, follows the same basic framework: pre-interview preparation, the interview itself, and the post-interview follow up. This fundamental trichotomy offers the skeleton around which the more specific elements of job interviews are arranged.

1. **Pre-Interview Preparation**: This phase forms the foundation of a successful job interview. It involves researching about the company, understanding the job role, identifying potential interview questions, and preparing concise but effective responses. It also entails preparing your resume, organizing important documents, and practicing interviews.

2. **The Interview Itself**: This is the performance phase, where candidates showcase their potential value to employers. It begins with the important first impression and includes aspects like body language, communication skills, problem-solving abilities, and cultural fit besides job-specific knowledge and skills.

3. **Post-Interview Follow Up**: Concluding the interview process on a positive note is as critical as the process itself. It involves sending a thank you note, seeking feedback, analyzing interview performance, and maintaining the connection made during the

interview.

2.2. The Pre-Interview Preparation

This phase is often overlooked, but it can be your secret weapon. When you know the company, its mission, its values, and its operations, you are better equipped to communicate how you can add value.

2.3. The Interview Itself

Resume Preparation, Document Organization, and Interviews Practices: *Tune your resume to match the role. Keep all required documents, certificates, and references organized. Practicing interviews with a peer can greatly improve your presentation skills.*

This is where you'll need to draw upon your preparation and perform.

2.4. The Post-Interview Follow-up

Cultural Fit: *Companies are not just looking for task-oriented employees; they want people who will mesh well with the workplace culture. Show your personality, showcase your alignment with company values, and articulate how you see yourself growing within the company.*

It's not over once you have walked out of the meeting room. The final phase involves maintaining a positive closure and building a relationship with your potential employer.

Maintaining the Connection: *Developing your professional network is a huge bonus from the job interviewing process. Keep in touch, approach them for advice, share interesting articles related to your field.*

By understanding the anatomy of a job interview, you can prepare effectively, perform confidently, and follow-up efficiently. This knowledge could mean the difference between simply doing an interview and acing it! Let's take this understanding forward and gear up for the next stage.

Chapter 3. Breaking Down Job Descriptions: Knowing What Employers Want

The first step in successfully navigating job interviews is understanding the prerequisites: the job descriptions. Deeply comprehending what employers want from their prospective employees is fundamental knowledge you should equip yourself with.

Before diving into the matter, it's important to underscore that job descriptions serve two primary purposes. Firstly, they detail the responsibilities and requirements of a specific role. Secondly, they serve as a tool to attract suitable candidates. While companies tend to aim for clarity in their job descriptions, they can often be filled with industry jargon or broad terminologies that might be puzzling. Cracking this code is your first task in the job-hunting process.

3.1. Decoding the Job Descriptions

Most job descriptions comprise several key sections: job title, job overview, responsibilities, qualifications, and traits or skills. By breaking down and analyzing each part, you'll have a clearer picture of what's expected in potential candidates.

1. **Job Title**: This usually represents a summary of the role. Be cautious not to overlook it. The job title reveals the level of experience required and gives cues about the nature of the role. Notice if it indicates a management position, a technical role, or a creative one.

2. **Job Overview**: This offers a snapshot of the role. It outlines the scope of the job and what you will be doing on an average day.

This will also probably tell you about the department and the team you would work with.

3. **Responsibilities**: This section defines your duties and what will be expected of you in the position. It helps you understand how your performance will be evaluated.

4. **Qualifications**: These are the must-haves to execute the job effectively. They typically include education, certifications, proficiency in specific skills, and years of relevant experience.

5. **Traits or Skills**: These are the intangible qualities that a successful candidate should possess. They reinforce ideas about company culture and values.

Exploring these segments will equip you with a clearer understanding of the expected skills, experience, and qualifications, enabling you to cater to your job applications accordingly.

3.2. Indicators of Company Culture

Observing subtler cues within a job description can reveal a lot about company culture. By picking up on nuances such as the tone and language used, or the emphasis placed on certain aspects, you can get a sense of what it would be like to work for the company.

Do they focus on teamwork or individual contribution? Are they conventional or innovative? Do they mention work-life balance or do they push for high-intensity performance? These distinctions can help you understand if you'd be a cultural fit and tailor your approach in the interview accordingly.

3.3. Matching Your Skills and Experience

Once you've decoded the job description and understood the

company culture, the next step is aligning your skills and experiences with what the job requires. Look for areas where your skills match those specified in the requirements. Highlight these in your resume and during the job interview.

Remember, not all skills have to be acquired professionally. Voluntary work, courses, or personal experiences where you developed relevant skills could be just as valuable. Be ready to reference specific examples during your interview to demonstrate your competencies.

3.4. Strategies for Handling Gaps in Your Skillset

Frequently, candidates may not align perfectly with every single requirement in a job description. Keep in mind, not all requirements are rigid; some flexibility may exist. If gaps appear, consider the following:

1. **Learn on the Job**: If the gap is in a learnable skill, emphasize your ability to quickly pick-up new skills.

2. **Transferable Skills**: Highlight related skills that can be applied in the required capacity.

3. **Demonstrate Willingness to Learn**: Showing enthusiasm to acquire a new skill can sometimes win you the role.

3.5. Conclusion

Decoding job descriptions requires patience, analytical skills, and a keen eye for detail. Once mastered, it can be an indispensable tool in your job hunting toolkit. By understanding what employers want, you position yourself as a strong competitor in the job market. And remember, keep an open mind. What you bring to the table might be just the fresh outlook a company needs, so be sure to communicate your unique value clearly throughout the application process.

This deep dive into dissecting job descriptions should equip you with the tools to set yourself up for success in any job application. Consistently practice this skill and you'll become adept at recognising not just what employers want, but also where you fit within the grand scheme of job opportunities. After all, the journey of successful employment is two-fold: finding the right job and being the right fit for it!

Chapter 4. Crafting a Compelling Resume and Cover Letter

Let's begin with understanding the main component of your job application – your resume. It acts as a snapshot of your professional history, skills, and accomplishments. Thus, it's essential that your resume is polished and compelling enough to catch the eye of an employer.

4.1. A. Structuring Your Resume

Standard resume structures usually comprise the following segments: Contact Information, Objective/Summary, Employment History, Skills, and Education. Let's dissect each section:

1. **Contact Information:** This is the header of your resume. Make sure to include your name, phone number, email address, and your LinkedIn profile (if applicable).

2. **Objective/Summary:** This section should be a brief overview of your professional goal and how you can contribute to the hiring company.

3. **Employment history:** List your previous job roles from most current to least, adding descriptions of your duties and accomplishments in bullet points.

4. **Skills:** Include hard skills and soft skills relevant to the job you are applying for.

5. **Education:** Highlight your academic qualifications in reverse chronological order. If you have any professional certifications, do include them here.

Remember, the way you present this information can vary based on whether you're using a chronological, functional, or hybrid resume type.

4.2. B. Crafting Impactful Job Descriptions

Creating influential job descriptions is all about showcasing the impact of your work. Here's how:

1. **Quantify your achievements:** Instead of saying "led a successful project", say "led a project team of 10 to deliver a software solution 2 weeks ahead of schedule, resulting in a 20% increase in efficiency".

2. **Use action verbs:** Phrases such as "implemented", "managed", or "transformed" depict your initiative.

3. **Tailor your descriptions:** Make sure your descriptions echo the language of the job description you're applying for. This way, your resume will resonate better with the recruiters.

4.3. C. Showcasing Relevant Skills

Skills should be relevant to the job you're applying for. For example, if you are applying for a role as a software engineer, your skills might include: coding languages you are well-versed with, software you have developed, or methodologies you have employed.

When it comes to showcasing soft skills, it's best to provide examples. Instead of merely including "team player" in your skills, you could say "collaborated with a team of 5 to deliver a project on time".

4.4. D. Effective Resume Design

The design of your resume should be professional and well-structured. Stick to one font family and include ample white space to make it easy to read. If you are in a creative field, a bit of color or graphics could leverage your chances, but keep it minimal and appealing.

4.5. E. Crafting Your Cover Letter

After the resume, comes the yet another crucial part of your job application - the cover letter. It's your first chance to communicate personally with the employer, express your interest in the job, and highlight how you are an excellent fit for the role.

Follow these tips to craft a compelling cover letter:

1. **Address it properly:** Avoid generic addresses like "To whom it may concern", instead, do a little research and address it to the relevant person.

2. **Showcase your research:** Mention what you admire about the company or how your skills align with the company's mission.

3. **Provide clear evidence:** Share instances from your past roles where you have leveraged your skills or brought about positive changes.

4. **Close professionally:** End on a positive note, showing your anticipation for the potential opportunity to discuss further.

Remember, your resume and cover letter are the first impressions you make on your potential employer. Invest time into crafting them well to ensure they showcase your capabilities effectively. With these tips, you're sure to make your application stand out!

Chapter 5. Acing Phone and Video Interviews: The New Normal

The advent of technology and the increasing need for convenient, remote hiring processes have given rise to a new form of job interview: phone and video calls. This format has its own set of rules, nuances, and tactics. While the principles of answering interview questions remain the same, their application in the context of remote interviews requires understanding and mindfulness.

5.1. Setting Up Your Space

Firstly, let's explore the critical aspect of setting up your space for the interview. Your environment plays a crucial role in ensuring a productive conversation, and minimising distractions is key. Find a quiet, well-lit room where you're unlikely to be interrupted. Ensure that your background is neutral and non-distracting. It's also vital to test your equipment prior to the interview to avoid technical glitches.

5.2. Testing Your Tech

Test your computer, headphones, internet connection, and video conferencing software well in advance of your interview. Additionally, keep your device's charger handy to avoid running out of power during the session. Ensure your microphone and camera are functioning correctly, and increase the clarity and sound quality by using a good quality headset instead of relying on your device's built-in components.

5.3. Dressing for Success

Just because you're interviewing from home doesn't mean you should skimp on your attire. Dress professionally as you would for an in-person interview. This not only helps to make a positive impression but also puts you in the right mindset. Avoid bright colors, intricate patterns, and jewelry that might cause distraction or reflection in the camera.

5.4. Body Language and Eye Contact

In video interviews, your body language and eye contact are crucial. Maintain a good posture by sitting up straight, leaning slightly forward to show engagement. Look at the camera, not the screen, to give the impression of eye contact. Use natural hand gestures, but avoid fidgeting or displaying nervous ticks, as these can be magnified on video.

5.5. Minimizing Distractions and Interruptions

Ensure that potential interruptions are minimized. Inform your household of your interview timings, put your phone on silent, and close any unrelated tabs or applications on your computer. Keeping your environment quiet and free from disturbances helps maintain the smooth flow of conversation and shows respect to your interviewer.

5.6. Mastering Audio Interviews

Telephone interviews are also a common first step in the hiring process. They come with their own set of considerations, which primarily revolve around voice and tone. Since visual cues are absent, convey your enthusiasm and confidence through your tone of voice.

Paying attention to your speech speed, intonation, and clarity is essential. Try standing up during your phone interview to help project enthusiasm and keep your energy levels high. Have a copy of your resume, the job advertisement, and any notes handy for easy reference during the conversation.

5.7. Building Rapport Virtually

Just like face-to-face interviews, building rapport is essential even in phone and video interviews. You can do this by showing enthusiasm for the role, asking insightful questions, and expressing your appreciation for the interviewer's time. Remember to smile, even in a phone interview, because it positively affects your tone of voice.

5.8. Post-Interview Etiquette

After the interview, send an email expressing your gratitude for the opportunity. This not only demonstrates your professionalism but also keeps you fresh in the interviewer's memory. Stay patient and composed while waiting for a response.

Navigating phone and video interviews can be daunting at first, but the right preparation and mindset can turn them into strengths. Remember that these formats are an opportunity to showcase your adaptability in an evolving virtual workforce. By understanding this 'New Normal' and acing these new interview formats, you open up a world of opportunities that transcends geographic boundaries and time zones. By mastering these strategies, not only will you gain confidence but also stand out as a strong candidate in your future phone and video interviews. The power to impress employers and land your dream job is well within your reach!

Chapter 6. Mind the Gap: Addressing Employment Gaps and Job Changes

Let's start by uncovering a reality: job applicants often worry about their employment history, mainly when they've experienced some periods of unemployment or frequent shifts between jobs. These phrases like "employment gaps" and "job hopping" can send chills down any job seeker's spine. However, remember, this does not have to be a factor that creates barriers in your career growth.

6.1. Deciphering Employment Gaps

Employment gaps are defined as periods of several months to a year or more between jobs where the job applicant has been unemployed. Typically, these are seen as red flags by hiring managers; however, the general perception has been changing roundly. The key is how you present these gaps and how effectively you communicate your activities during those periods.

6.2. Reasons Behind Employment Gaps

There can be multitudinous reasons for employment gaps, and it's important to articulate these reasons honestly and effectively. The most common reasons can include layoffs or company downsizing, personal or family health issues, spending time as a stay-at-home parent, sabbaticals, going back to school, or simply taking time to travel or explore one's interests. By explaining the reason behind these gaps upfront, you build an atmosphere of trust and understanding.

6.3. Framing Your Story

The way you frame your story regarding the employment gap can make a crucial difference. Here's where you can turn the gap into an asset:

1. **Skills Acquired:** Talk about the skills you learned and how they can benefit the potential job. It could have been a certification course, volunteering work, or any other skill enhancer.

2. **Projects Undertaken:** If you worked as a freelancer or contractor during your gap, mentioning these projects can showcase the effective utilization of your time and skills.

3. **Personal Growth:** If your break was due to personal reasons, focus on the positive outcomes of your personal journey, such as increased resilience, improved interpersonal abilities, and better stress management.

6.4. Addressing Job Changes

Employment gaps aren't the only potential stumbling blocks; frequent changes in jobs or "job hopping" can also raise eyebrows in potential employers.

6.5. Unraveling Job Changes

Job hopping refers to changing jobs very frequently, typically every one to two years. This can give an impression of instability or disloyalty. However, there's an art to making this frequent movement work in your favor.

6.6. Reasons Behind Job Changes

The reasons behind frequent job changes can be quite varied. Maybe you were looking for a better fit, seeking increased pay or exploring different industries. Perhaps it was due to personal situations, like relocating for a partner or reevaluating priorities post-pandemic.

6.7. Making Job Changes Work for You

1. **Highlighting Skill Growth:** Emphasize the diverse skills and experiences you picked up in each role. Show your potential employer how these skills can add value to their team.

2. **Relationship Management:** Talk about the good relations you've maintained with all your past employers. References can come as aid.

3. **Resilience:** Showcase how your job changes highlight your adaptability and resilience. This can potentially make you more attractive in industries where change is constant, like technology or marketing.

Let's conclude by emphasizing that being honest is crucial when addressing employment gaps and job changes. However, it's how you frame these circumstances that can turn potential red flags into green. Remember, everyone has a unique career path with ups, downs, twists, and turns. Your journey, gaps and all, is a part of who you are as a professional, and there's no reason why it should hinder your future growth.

Chapter 7. Behavioral Interviews: Telling Your Story Effectively

In the job interview sphere, knowing how to effectively tell your story during a behavioral interview is paramount. It determines whether the interviewer perceives you as just another face or as the candidate they've been searching for. Herein, we break down effective strategies to ensure your behavioral interview is an absolute success.

7.1. Understanding Behavioral Interviews

To tell your story effectively in a behavior interview, you first need to understand what a behavioral interview is and why employers use it. Behavioral interviews are based on the psychology principle that past behavior is the most accurate indicator of future performance. During such interviews, you'll be asked to provide examples of how you've handled situations related to the job you're applying for. Behavioral interviews go beyond what's on your resume to reveal how you handle tasks and solve problems.

7.2. Why Behavioral Interviews Matter

Unlike traditional interview questions that focus on theoretical responses to hypothetical scenarios, behavioral interviews provide employers with insights into how you have operated in real-life situations. They shine a spotlight on your skills, abilities, and personality, providing an excellent opportunity to show your value and potential contribution to the potential employer.

7.3. Preparing for Behavioral Interviews

Just like any other type of interview, preparation is key for success in behavioral interviews. Think of instances where you dealt with challenging situations, showed initiative, managed a team, or solved a complex problem. Don't forget smaller successes; sometimes, they reveal the most about your character. Remember, employers want to hire people who can not only get the job done but also fit in with their team and company culture.

To help you identify ideal situations to share, use the STAR (Situation, Task, Action, Result) format.

- **Situation**: Describe the context or setting where the action took place.
- **Task**: State the challenge or problem you faced.
- **Action**: Talk about the steps you took to address the challenge.
- **Result**: Finally, discuss the outcomes of your actions.

When using the STAR response method, be as detailed as possible. Your goal is to paint a vivid picture that makes it easy for the employer to envision you as part of their team.

7.4. Conducting a Self-Assessment

Before going to your behavioral interview, it's important to conduct a thorough self-assessment. This will help you to understand your strengths and weaknesses and how they relate to the job you're applying for. Knowing your areas of strength and weakness can help you prepare for behavioral interview questions related to them.

For instance, if you are applying for a leadership role and know that decision-making is a strength, prepare anecdotes about the times you made difficult decisions and what the outcome was. Conversely, if you have trouble staying organized, think of an instance when your weakness was exposed and discuss how you're working to improve it.

7.5. During the Interview

Making a positive first impression during the behavioral interview is crucial. Dress professionally, make eye contact with the interviewer, and remain calm and composed even under pressure. If you find it challenging to recall instances on the spot, try to visualize your past experiences before the interview. Recall the feelings, actions, conversations, and outcomes. This will make it easier to share these experiences during the interview.

7.6. Post-Interview Follow-Up

After the behavioral interview, do a post-interview analysis. Did you omit any crucial information? Were there any gaps in your storytelling? Reflecting on your interview performance will help you identify areas for improvement and prepare you for future interviews.

Lastly, remember to thank the interviewer for their time and the opportunity to interview. It shows respect for their time and reinforces your interest in the job. Email or handwritten notes are both acceptable forms of expressing your gratitude.

In conclusion, navigating behavioral interviews takes practice and self-awareness. With preparation, introspection, and the right storytelling skills, you can excel in behavioral interviews and make remarkable impressions on potential employers. Your ability to turn past experiences into compelling narratives is a key step towards

landing your dream job. Keep practicing, keep improving, and your
efforts will pay off!

Chapter 8. Technical Interviews: Demonstrate Your Skills

Technical interviews are a unique space where the primary focus shifts to your technical skills, abilities, and knowledge. This presents a distinctive opportunity to showcase what you know and to illustrate to your potential employers that you can deliver the goods.

8.1. Understanding Technical Interviews

Different to other forms of interviews, technical interviews primarily test the specific professional skills required for the job role. The objective is to assess your technical knowledge, problem-solving abilities, and understanding of principles related to the job. These could involve coding problems for a developer interview, system designing for an architecture role, or diagnostic questions for a service technician position.

Typically, employers value the process and the logic you apply to solve a problem rather than just the final solution. The interview may also involve behavioral questions to examine your team skills, approach to failure, handling of work pressures, or mentoring abilities.

8.2. How to Prepare for a Technical Interview

A systematic approach is essential to succeed in technical interviews.

1. Start by reviewing the job description or role profile to understand the technical skills needed.

2. Identify the technologies, languages, and toolkits that are crucial to the job.

3. Brush up on your basic principles and concepts related to the technologies.

4. Practice problem-solving involving these concepts. There are several websites available for this.

5. Try explaining technical concepts to a non-technical person. If you can explain it to them, you understand it.

6. Learn about the company and its work culture. Often interviews include culture-fit questions.

Remember, you don't need to know everything. Demonstrating a growth mindset and the ability to learn is just as important as showcasing your current knowledge.

8.3. During The Technical Interview

During the interview, be conscious of your communication, problem-solving approach, and clarity of thoughts. Here are some tips to ensure you make an optimum impact:

1. Listen carefully to the question before jumping to an answer.

2. If you are unsure of what's asked, clarify. Don't assume.

3. Walk the interviewer through your thought process. This will serve two purposes. Firstly, it opens up a dialogue and transforms the interview into a discussion. Secondly, it gives the interviewer a view of your problem-solving skills.

4. It's okay to say "I don't know". But always follow it up with how you would find the solution.

5. Ensure you discuss both, the strengths and potential limitations

of your solution.

8.4. Handling Coding Questions

For engineering roles and developers, coding questions are an integral part of technical interviews. The best approach to tackling these is to:

1. Understand and clarify the problem. Never assume.

2. Plan your solution logically before starting to code. Always communicate your approach before writing code.

3. While you code, communicate the critical steps, so the interviewer follows along.

4. Once done, review your solution for any errors or possible improvements.

You may also be given an existing piece of code and asked to debug or enhance it. This is to ascertain your skills to collaborate on a pre-existing project.

8.5. System Design Questions

Primarily for architecture roles and senior developer positions, system design questions are designed to test your knowledge and judgement regarding architectural principles and system behaviors.

1. Like any other problem, first, understand the requirements clearly.

2. Draw a high-level design showing key components of your solution.

3. Discuss your design with the interviewer before going into details.

4. Once agreed on high-level design, discuss how the components

will talk to each other.

5. Discuss trade-offs and alternatives you would consider if you had more resources or time.

Remember, design questions might not always have a single correct answer. Interviewers are more interested in your thought process, rationale for choosing a design, and your ability to think in an abstract manner.

8.6. Behavioural Questions

Don't forget that the technical interview is still part of a job interview, and your attitude and behavior are as essential as your technical skills.

1. Be enthusiastic about the role and your work.

2. Show that you can work well within a team. Illustrate it with examples.

3. Display a learning mindset. Discuss the last technology you learned or a project problem that made you learn something new.

4. Be prepared to discuss scenarios involving failure, conflict, or dealing with pressure. Show resilience in your responses.

Prepare for these questions using the STAR method - Situation, Task, Action, Result. It helps to structure your responses effectively.

8.7. In Review

Technical interviews can seem daunting, but with the right preparation, you can fare well. Anticipate the scenarios, practice problem solving, and most importantly, be yourself. Your personality and attitude, combined with technical skills, can charm the interviewer and land you the job.

Remember, the fundamental idea of the technical interview is not just to quiz you on your knowledge, but to understand how you apply this knowledge to problems. Can you think logically and systematically? Can you adapt and learn? This is what makes the difference.

In the following chapters, we will delve deeper into these aspects, discuss some common myths surrounding technical interviews, and review strategies to ace your next one. Ensure to grasp the knowledge shared and, more importantly, use it in the practical world to ensure you stand tall in your technical interviews!

Let the technical interview be a platform to present your skills, your zeal, and your readiness to learn and grow in your professional journey.

Chapter 9. Negotiating Job Offers: Knowing Your Worth

A job offer is often a cause of either jubilation or a sense of deflation. If it's the former, it's because the compensation, position, and company align perfectly with your career goals. If it's the latter, it's likely because there's a disconnect between your expectations and what's on the offer letter. In such a scenario, negotiation is key. However, negotiation is often a daunting prospect because of the fear of appearing 'greedy' or the apprehension of losing the offer entirely. This is why it's crucial to navigate the negotiation process carefully, effectively, and strategically.

To this end, let's break down this process into five key components:

9.1. Understanding Your Worth

The first and most important step in any negotiation process is understanding your worth. This doesn't mean having an inflated sense of self-importance, but rather, an objective understanding of one's value based on skills, experiences, and contributions.

Recall your achievements, added values, and key contributions in your past role. Convert them into tangible figures or results. These will play a prominent role in demonstrating your professional value. Use tools such as Glassdoor, LinkedIn Salary Insights, and Payscale to research average salaries in your industry, city, and position. Compare their compensation range with your preferred one.

9.2. Building Your Case

Once you've established a value range, it's time to build a case to justify this. This involves quantifying the impact of your work and achievements and translating it into a clear, concise narrative.

For example, instead of just stating you "led a team," you could say, "I led a team of five, achieving a 25% increase in project efficiency, leading to an annual saving of $50,000." The latter provides exact figures that demonstrate your value.

9.3. The Thorough Pre-Negotiation Preparation

Being prepared is key to negotiation success. First, be emotionally ready. Any negotiation process is bound to be filled with counterarguments, potential for conflict, and need for compromise. Be prepared for this, stay calm, and maintain a positive attitude throughout.

Next, gather data. Arm yourself with salaries, growth opportunities, benefits, and industry standards aligned with your role on the negotiation table. Additionally, understanding the financial health, market position, and growth forecasts of the company could provide you with a valuable context. Knowledge is power, and data is your ammunition in negotiation.

9.4. Planning Your Negotiation Strategy

Next, plan your negotiation strategy. Openly discuss salary expectations during the earlier stages of the job application process, ensuring neither party wastes time. During discussions, use the evidence you've collated to argue your case for a higher salary. Always give a salary range rather than a fixed figure.

During conversations, it's also crucial to initially focus on salary and then talk about other benefits. This order is essential because your overall compensation depends significantly on your base salary. Be sure to understand that every component of the offer is potentially negotiable, decreasing negotiation apprehension and increasing the potential compensation you can receive.

9.5. Driving a Hard, but Respectful Bargain

Finally, during the actual negotiation, remember to drive a hard bargain, but be respectful. While negotiating, start at the top of your salary range. This gives you room to handle counteroffers. However, ensure that your range is justified by the industry standards, the company's offering, and most importantly, your skill set and experience.

Negotiating job offers is an art, one that you will get better at with practice. Be patient, stay composed, and be persistent. Remember that negotiation is a two-way street. It's not just about what you get; it's also about ensuring that the deal works for your prospective employer.

Remember, you're negotiating not just for more, but for what you're worth. The first salary negotiation might feel awkward, but it's worth it. It sets the stage for your future growth within the company and possibly, your career. So don't undervalue yourself. As long as you're respectful and clear in your negotiation, you're on the right path. Use this guidance to structure your approach, and the process will become much smoother.

Chapter 10. Turning Rejections into Opportunities: Post-interview Reflections

Ever experienced a job interview rejection that left you devastated and questioning your worth? Most of us have walked that path once, if not more. It's crucial to remember: rejections do not define your abilities or potential. They are merely bumpers on your journey to the right job fit. This section will teach you how to turn these stumbling blocks into stepping stones.

10.1. The Reflection Stage

Taking the time to reflect after rejection is critical. It might not be an immediate instinct to question why it happened. In fact, this can be an emotionally taxing effort. However, this reflection provides invaluable insights.

Firstly, don't disregard your emotions. It's merited to feel disappointed, even frustrated. Nonetheless, avoid personalizing the rejection. It's beneficial to give yourself time to process it rather than rush yourself into a space of forced positivity.

10.2. Glean Insights from Feedback

Most employers provide feedback post-interview. If they don't, it's wholly appropriate to ask for it. Here's how to request feedback correctly:

- Don't demand. Ask kindly.

- Make it apparent that you seek an opportunity for growth and improvement.

- If feedback hasn't been offered, you may phrase your request like: "I appreciate the opportunity to interview for [position]. To enhance my skills and performance, could you provide some feedback on my interview?".

Now, deciphering feedback deserves caution. Extract the constructive criticism and strive to implement it. If the feedback includes aspects you cannot alter or seems unfair, reflect on whether such an organization aligns with your values.

10.3. Analyzing Your Performance

After receiving feedback, do a comprehensive performance self-review. Here are some aspects to consider:

1. Resume and Cover Letter: Evaluate your resume. Is it tailored to the job you applied for? Does it highlight relevant skills, accomplishments and experiences? Likewise, review your cover letter. Highlight skills that align with the job description, relevancy is a key factor.

2. First Impression: Did you dress appropriately? Were you punctual? How confident did you feel and portray?

3. Communication Skills: Did you speak clearly and articulate your points well? Observe your body language.

4. Interview Answers: Revisit your responses. Were they concise and relevant?

5. Questions Asked: Did you ask insightful questions about the company and role?

10.4. Building a Corrective Action Plan

Once you've done a thorough analysis, it's time to create a corrective action plan. This will help you address identified weaknesses systematically.

- Define Objectives: What are you aiming to improve? Be specific.

- Develop an Action Plan: How will you achieve these objectives? It could be professional development courses, workshops, or seeking a mentor for guidance.

- Set Time Frames: Implementing a change isn't immediate. Set a chronology for your action steps.

- Regular Assessment: Have regular check-ins. Are your strategies working? Adjust them if you're not seeing progress.

10.5. Embracing Rejections as Opportunities

Remember, every rejection you encounter brings you closer to your perfect job fit. It teaches you more about your strengths, weaknesses, and, ultimately, about you as an individual. More importantly, it helps you limit the gap between where you are and where you want to be. Let rejections pave your path to personal growth and professional development.

Rejections can be demoralizing and sometimes you may even want to throw in the towel. Be patient and persistent. Tenacity is a virtue highly valued in any competitive professional landscape. Let your application rejections serve as building blocks for a stronger, more resilient you - perfectly primed and ready to seize the right opportunity when it comes along.

This exercise of post-interview reflection and turning rejections into opportunities is essentially one of personality building, resilience strengthening, and skill enhancing. Once you adopt this approach, no setback will seem unsurmountable. So the next time you receive a "no", let it motivate you rather than deflate you, letting your story of struggle render you all the more attractive to your future dream employers.

Remember, it's not about the destination but the journey that defines your success. Each rejection you face is just a stepping stone towards finding the perfect fit. Such is the road to self-improvement: defeats become triumphs and criticisms pave the path to excellence. So, let the strength of your spirit get fueled by the spark of rejection, and embrace the resolute power that lies within you. Let's turn rejections into stepping stones towards your dream job!

Chapter 11. Keeping Up Your Momentum: Staying Motivated in Your Job Search

Your journey to landing your dream job is akin to running a marathon, a test of endurance that demands grit, determination, and sustained momentum. Keeping up your morale and staying motivated throughout this journey, especially during periods of rejection or prolonged job hunting, can be challenging. However, it is crucial for your ultimate success. Maintaining momentum in your job search doesn't only keep you committed to the goal but also puts you in an advantageous position when opportunities arise.

11.1. Developing A Positive Mindset

A positive mindset is a prerequisite to sustaining motivation during your job-hunting journey. Your thought pattern significantly influences your outlook, affecting your decision-making process and the way you react to situations. If you consistently harbor negative thoughts, such as the fear of rejection or inadequacy, they can send your motivation spiraling.

To combat these, regularly practice positive affirmations and visualization techniques. Envision yourself successfully nailing job interviews, receiving job offers, and thriving in your desired role. These methods will infuse a confidence boost and push you forward in your job search.

11.2. Setting Finite, Achievable Goals

Breaking down your job search into numerous small, achievable goals can make the entire process seem less overwhelming. Instead of a broad objective like 'Find a job in three months,' opt for smaller, more measurable targets such as 'Send out five resumes per week' or 'Connect with two new professionals in my field every day.'

Celebrating each little accomplishment not just feeds into your sense of progress, but also helps keep the momentum going. Reaching these small milestones creates a sense of success, thus, promoting a positive feedback loop that encourages further action.

11.3. Staying Organized

An organized job search is an effective one. Keeping track of where you are in the application process with different companies can seem daunting when trying to manage everything in your head. Develop a system for tracking job applications to help stay organized and reduce stress. You could use a spreadsheet or job search apps — tools which allow you to document important details about each job posting, track the application status, and set reminders for follow-ups.

Besides, scheduling specific time blocks dedicated solely to your job search can help maintain focus and increase efficiency. Incorporate break periods to prevent burnout and allow for rejuvenation.

11.4. Continuous Learning and Skill Development

Keep yourself engaged in continuous learning and skill development activities, such as taking up relevant online courses, attending webinars and workshops, or reading industry-based books. This ongoing professional development uplifts your morale by making you feel proactive and productive, even when you're yet to land a job. These measures also enhance your qualifications and make you a more attractive candidate to prospective employers.

11.5. Expanding Your Network

Networking goes a long way in assisting your job search. Not only does this diversify your job sources, but conversations and interactions with industry professionals can also provide insider knowledge about the job market, encouraging your job-hunting spirit. Remember, every conversation could open doors to unforeseen opportunities.

Moreover, the satisfaction derived from developing valuable relationships and widening your professional bearings contributes positively to your pursuit. Using platforms like LinkedIn for networking and joining relevant professional groups can fuel your job searching momentum.

11.6. Maintaining Physical and Mental Health

During the job search, it's easy to neglect self-care and let stress get the best of us. However, maintaining a balanced diet, regular exercise regimen, and adequate sleep routine helps in boosting overall mood and energy levels. Incorporating mindful practices like meditation or yoga into your daily routine can also ward off stress and keep your motivation up.

Staying mentally calm and physically fit ensures that you're in the best possible condition when opportunities for interviews come around—raising the odds of impressing potential employers.

11.7. Embracing Rejection

Rejection is an integral part of a job search, but not an end. Instead of getting disheartened by unfruitful results, use them as stepping stones towards your ultimate goal. Each "No" brings you closer to the "Yes" you're aiming for. Feedback, if any, from unsuccessful interviews can be invaluable to identify areas of improvement and refine your approach in future interviews.

Remember, maintaining momentum demands constant effort and a positive attitude. Your determination and patience through this marathon will eventually reward you with your coveted prize - landing your dream job. So keep on moving, keep on striving, and keep on shining; your perseverance will, without a doubt, pay off!